PANGOLIN

LONDON

BEING HERE

A RETROSPECTIVE VIEW OF THE WORK OF WILLIAM TUCKER

An outstretched palm holds a copy of the *Willendorf Venus*. The hand belongs to William Tucker and the black-and-white photograph – the cover of a magazine edited by Tucker at St Martin's in 1961 – has often been reproduced in the context of his work. For some, clearly, it presages the direction Tucker later adopted in his own sculpture. With hindsight, however, a more apposite reading can be made of this archaic and enigmatic figure passing into the hand of this particular artist. For just as the 20,000-year-old 'Venus' resists definitive interpretation, so Tucker's subsequent evolution as a sculptor has eluded simple categorisation. Yet it is precisely through embracing this potential for slippage, and, above all, by refuting any closed reading, that his work has maintained its identity and independence over fifty years of development.

In beginning this short introduction, I intended to avoid interpretation (although inevitably I failed). My initial observation, however, is limited to noting that the sculpture of William Tucker simply exists. Or rather, that it signifies its existence *overtly*. And in so doing it identifies with that long philosophical enquiry into phenomenology, from Plato's cave to Merleau-Ponty: a concern with the 'thing-in-itself' to borrow Kant's term. And this is rather remarkable. Our natural predisposition is to categorise. Concepts clarify the world, but often it is only the initial moment of confrontation that yields any intimation of the existence of the thing-in-itself, naked and unadorned by its conceptual baggage.

The estrangement associated with that primary encounter has remained fundamental to Tucker's sculpture, from the steel, aluminium and fibreglass works of the 1960s to the monumental bronzes produced since the eighties. Working in series, his sculpture has progressed through radically different media, forms and references, yet has always retained the essential ability to confront, confuse and disarm our expectations, and so return us time and again to the sculpture's objecthood.

Although Tucker was born in Cairo in 1935, his formative years were spent in the UK. During the postwar decade, the influence of French Existentialism

Greek Horse
2003, Bronze
Edition of 4
142.2 cm high

(with its own debts to the phenomenology of Heidegger), and an awareness
of the Holocaust, the atomic bomb and the Cold War, all found a resonance
in art being produced on both sides of the Channel. Yet by the time Tucker
began making sculpture, the focus was already shifting in the direction of
Pop and its engagement with commercial design, mass production and
transient fashion. It was a shift of galactic proportions, the collision between
a Europe steeped in a humanist tradition and the brash, disenfranchised
immediacy of America.

The St Martin's sculptors – seen as successors to Anthony Caro and
including David Annesley, Michael Bolus, Philip King, Tim Scott, Isaac Witkin
and Tucker himself – were central to this new milieu. Their work, already in
the public sphere by 1962, was celebrated by Bryan Robertson's milestone
New Generation exhibition in 1965 and blessed by the high priest of modernism,
Clement Greenberg. Tucker was included in *documenta IV* in 1968 and
represented Britain at the *Venice Biennale* in 1972, while continuing as a
teacher whose influence has been widely acknowledged by a later generation
of St Martin's students that included Richard Deacon and Bill Woodrow.

Tucker's work from the earlier sixties could be mistaken for Pop, although
it owed more to the impact of American abstract painting, the first extensive
showing of which had finally reached London in 1959. Shortly after it was

Series A No. V
1968, Fibreglass
Unique
58 cm high

mistaken for Minimal art and included in the seminal *Primary Structures* exhibition (New York, 1966), alongside Andre, Judd, LeWitt and Morris. It shared the cool detachment of Pop and Minimalism, but any identification with those movements was at best a manifestation of what Raymond Williams termed the 'structure of feeling', the commonalities that permeate and characterise particular eras. Tucker explored the design-like forms, contemporary materials and clean colours of Pop, and the repetition of simple, industrial-like elements axiomatic to Minimal art, but both movements were endgames and fundamentally reductionist. And Tucker was neither.

As his work continued to evolve, it was never possible to identify the definitive signature piece. Each series marked a new departure, the basic elements seeming to mutate in unexpected directions, constantly confronting audiences with the unknown, with forms that acknowledged their own estrangement.

But this is only half the story, because beyond the formal aesthetics of an abstract vocabulary lay the figurative ghost in the machine. At times it was only a question of scale that suggested the human presence or a sensuously curved form suggestive of a body-part. At others, as with *Series A*, it was the coupling of elements, like spent lovers striking a languorous pose. Or, as in the *Cat's Cradle* series, it was the spidery elements tracing three-dimensional paths in the air as if an innovative form of dance notation. Or the later *Beulah* series, with its suggestion of a more urgent, animalistic writhing. I am not suggesting these as interpretations, even less as the artist's intentions, but as indications of what we might intuit as a point of contact: an empathy that identifies with tradition and distinguishes these strange, elusive forms from other objects that populate our world.

(RIGHT)
Cat's Cradle I
1971, Stainless Steel
Unique
112 cm high

(FAR RIGHT)
Beulah I
1971, Steel
Unique
151.1 cm

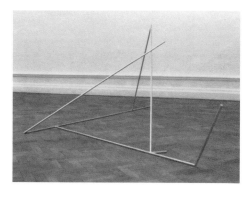
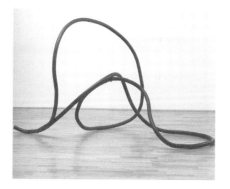

(TOP LEFT)
Tunnel
1975, Laminated
Masonite
Unique
213 cm high

(LEFT)
House
1975, Oak
Unique
229 cm high

Because, in the end, William Tucker is a traditionalist, and has never abandoned history as a resource and a point of reference. An awareness of that accumulated weight is evident in many of the titles (Tucker took Classics and read History at Oxford before studying art, and at various times has performed as critic, author and curator). But, as with the *Willendorf Venus*, historical precedents are never without their ambiguities. History, and in particular mythology, offers multiple readings. And so the lifeline the artist throws us becomes more of a Gordian knot. Are we being directed to classical antiquity or alerted to its mirror-like palimpsest accrued through centuries of interpretation and re-reading? Or perhaps to that great faker of antiquity, Michelangelo, whose unfinished Slaves for the tomb of Julian II serve as the perfect metaphor for the human condition and for the animate within the inanimate.

All of the above, I suspect, but while these concerns were no more than mooted in the early works, they really came into their own from the mid-seventies, and particularly following the artist's move to New York in 1978. *Tunnel* and *House* (both 1975), and monumental figures such as *The Promise*, *Sphinx*, *Carytid* and *Ouranos*, executed in the first half of the eighties, marked the gradual transition into what would become his current work, dominated by organic or anthropomorphic modelled forms cast in bronze. In these we find the ultimate meeting of the object – the solid, unyielding casts with their undeniable presence – and the fleeting reverberations of history: a synthesis between Michael Fried's ahistorical objecthood and the European tradition from which, ironically, Tucker himself was now geographically estranged.

A fellow traveller from that European tradition who is worth mentioning is the Catalan artist, Antoni Tàpies. Like Tucker, Tàpies celebrates the thing-in-itself, most especially in the 'matter paintings', where he mythologises the 'base' object, drawing on the potential of inert material to stimulate associations of a more complex socio-cultural dimension (to which we might add spiritual, ecological, historical, philosophical... and a catalogue of other concerns both artists share).

But this leads us to question the degree to which art is capable of transmitting such subtle complexities. The Chinese, for example, traditionally venerate rocks from Tai Hu, in whose 'natural' forms they perceive entire landscapes; fantasies of the unconscious. The rocks have been carefully selected, sculpted, then weathered by immersion in rivers, but essentially they remain random starting points for meditation. If Tucker's sculpture functions in a similar vein, then we might ask to what extent does the artist determine our responses? Or is our interpretation simply arbitrary?

To answer this, we have first to acknowledge that *any* artist, unless overly literary, only goes so far in dictating our reading of the work; that inevitably there remains a distance between author and reader. As T. S. Elliot puts it, 'between the idea and the reality... falls the shadow'. But this gap is by no means negative, granting the viewer ultimate responsibility for determining how the work is received. In his sculpture, Tucker sets the scene, creating the situation for confrontation. He steers us through myriad subtle clues, drawing on the common language of the past. And he disarms our preconceptions by emphatically stating that what stands before us is primarily an object rooted in the physical world, simultaneously accepting and withstanding any reading we care to place upon it. Beyond that it is up to us.

*   *   *

The current show both exposes a selection of work produced over the past sixteen years and celebrates the more recent relationship between the artist and Pangolin Editions. The foundry has cast all the exhibited works, a process that demands a close collaboration between the sculptor and the technical skills of the foundry team, from the translation of the original plaster or clay into bronze, to the intricacies of finishing and patination.

Confronting these works, initially we might be struck by the incongruity of Tucker's emphatic use of bronze, while *apparently* challenging the status of this most traditional of materials. Above all, bronze implies permanence and stability. Amorphous and organic, these immutable objects appear to be in a

(TOP LEFT)
The Promise
1980, Concrete
Unique
290 cm high

(TOP RIGHT)
Sphinx
1980, Wood
Unique
487.7 cm high

paradoxical condition of flux, of becoming: an arrested state between being and nothingness, a confluence of object and idea. For while the evocation of sculpture's past is anything but overt, an awareness of such precedents undeniably informs our perception. A tension exists between the actuality of the sculpture-as-object and the more ephemeral associations it provokes, a constant oscillation between the two poles of 'seeing' and 'seeing as'.

Messenger (2001), for example, first appears as a towering outcrop, a natural form ravaged by the elements. We might then become engrossed in the multifaceted detailing of the surface and the gentle nuances of the patina, its graduated tones modulating and softening the form, suggesting a slow weathering with the accumulated verdigris of some copper-rich mineral. So it comes as a surprise when we find ourselves reading the suggestion of toes at the sculpture's base. After a second's indecision, we stand back and, in changing position, witness the entire bronze transform into an enormous foot, shorn off above the ankle. While a moment before we were *seeing* a material object, that same object is now *seen as* a muscled foot, straining and poised to take flight.

Consider, also, *Greek Horse* (2003) and the similar metamorphosis of this skyward-reaching – and seemingly abstract – sculpture as it transforms into a gaping, equestrian head: for all its ambiguities, the reference is intended. Or the deceptively titled *Cave* (2005), the eponymous opening – a nod to both Plato's cave and the novel by José Saramago – at first appearing in what

resembles a rock wall, but which on further reading resolves itself into a giant fist, clenched and severed at the wrist. And again, *Emperor* (2002) with its profile of a reclining human head recumbent on the ground as if slain in battle. Or, on a slightly smaller scale, the ambiguity of the corporeal reference that might be glimpsed in *Siren* (1994), steering us through its sand-coloured patina to the many fractured limbs and torsos surviving from antiquity.

Naturally, there is no *a priori* value to these works evoking this catalogue of body-parts: it is not that these anthropomorphic masses somehow lay claim to a higher order of sculpture simply by virtue of being figurative. (On the other hand, by far the greater part of sculpture's past *has* depicted the human figure, and so history itself is not exactly unbiased!) Yet Tucker's approach to the figurative is not quite as direct as it might seem. Although all of these works belong to series in which the artist has pursued specific figurative references in depth, revealingly the image in every case originated by chance through the construction of purely abstract forms. On occasions, these have even evolved out of discarded shards of plaster culled from the studio floor.

Why, then, pursue – often over a considerable number of years – what was in effect a chance occurrence? The answer almost certainly lies in our unconscious affinity for significant forms (as distinct from Clive Bell's notion of significant *form*); specifically forms whose significance has been defined and underscored through sculpture's long history, and which retain their significance even when sited on the cusp of abstraction. Note that Tucker implicitly rejects the teleological model (that of progress over time), instead regarding all sculpture as belonging to one undifferentiated, non-hierarchical collectivity, through which we can intuit those forms that have, over aeons, achieved ascendency.

Through reworking and refinement, what initially was intuitively grasped is brought within reach of consciousness, although never actually thrust beyond its threshold. To this end Tucker has pursued these forms relentlessly, both in sculpture and in drawings and monoprints (a number of which are included in this exhibition and should be viewed as works in their own right). He has tracked his forms to source, at times finding confirmation in the Parthenon frieze, the monolithic figures of Pharaonic Egypt, or in any number of more recent masters from Michelangelo to Rodin; even in the work of his nearer-contemporaries, as in his 1974 survey, *The Language of Sculpture* – a personal reflection on the early development of the modernist school that remains in print to this day.

Messenger
2001, Bronze
Edition of 3
320 cm high

But these historical models are not in themselves the progenitors of Tucker's work. Rather, it is the aggregate of sculpture's long history that favours the prepared mind, suggesting – without specificity – what brief notations might most succinctly evoke the cornerstones and bedrock of that history.

There are exceptions. This exhibition also includes a number of smaller sculptures modelled after specific works by Degas and Matisse. One represents a dancer, another a seated figure. But it would be an astute viewer that could identify the original. Even if one could, the address goes beyond the particular to the general notion of sculpture: its forms, traditions and conventions. In these and other smaller works included here, we are invited to address that unique relationship with scale existing between the sculptural object and the viewer. These smaller works cry out to be held, proposing an indexical relation to the human hand. Like the *Willendorf Venus*, they invite a tactile response: not only to reach a measure of their compact mass, but to retrace the forms left by the artist's fingers in the original clay or by the tools used to model the plaster – the physicality of the work as object.

Let's sum up what's happening here. Initially, we are confronted with the material substance of the sculpture: its scale (whether large or small), its form, the intricacies of the surface modelling and patina. Admittedly, it is quite possible we don't progress beyond this, or at least not consciously. But if we do, we may begin to discern a figurative reference that asserts itself through the process of looking. This may suggest associations with the work of other artists, and beyond that with the wider history and tradition of sculpture itself. But always within these perceptions lies the sculpture's essential materiality. The invitation is to see beyond any associations proper to the piece, restoring the sculpture to its primary status of objecthood; but an object with loaded significance. At one and the same time we can, conceptually at least, hold the notion of it being both object and signifier, something solipsistic but which nevertheless points to an unbounded set of references beyond itself.

Tucker's work today clearly stands aside from the mainstream of our times. Yet, by virtue of this distancing, and through its appeal to a multilayered universality, it succeeds in becoming not only more relevant in itself, but more relevant to what sculpture *might* be: suggesting not so much the *condition* of sculpture, as its *potential*. If Tucker's work holds a 'message' for contemporary audiences it is that 'presence' and 'tangibility' – the awareness of 'being here' – constitutes a more substantive relationship to the world than the condition of dislocation implicit in today's digitally-based information culture: that to know the world is not the same as experiencing it.

Tucker is represented in public collections worldwide – including MoMA, the Guggenheim and Metropolitan, New York; Tate; the National Gallery of Australia; etc. – and in April, coinciding with this show, he will receive a lifetime achievement award from the International Sculpture Center, joining an exclusive list of past recipients including Bourgeois, Caro, Chillida, Oldenburg, Paik, Rauschenberg and Segal. Nevertheless, it would be disingenuous to deny this is difficult, challenging work, far removed from the one-liner signature pieces of many of today's younger sculptors. But no one said art had to be easy. In its rigorous interrogation of what it means to make art at this moment, Tucker might put us in mind of John Cage. Cage's struggle to make noise and above all silence – the two irreducible components of music – acceptable to audiences has still not been universally won. Radio broadcasters refer to silence as 'dead air'. What Tucker is trying to make us accept is dead weight: mass. But of course it isn't dead, any more than Cage's silences. Both are filled with their/our own inner life, both entire worlds within Blake's metaphorical grain of sand.

KEITH PATRICK
Barcelona, 2010

Emperor
2002, Bronze
Edition of 5
165.1 cm high

CATALOGUE

Chryseis
1993, Bronze
Edition of 4
76.2 cm high

Study for Odalisque
2008, Bronze
Edition of 10
10.2 cm high

(LEFT)
After Matisse II
2008, Sterling Silver
Edition of 10
7 cm high

(ABOVE)
After Matisse I
2008, Sterling Silver
Edition of 10
7 cm high

Study for
'Emperor'
2002, Bronze
Edition of 6
12 cm high

Cave
2005, Plaster
for Bronze
Edition of 3
147.3 cm high

Study for 'Cave'
2004, Bronze
Edition of 6
9.5 cm high

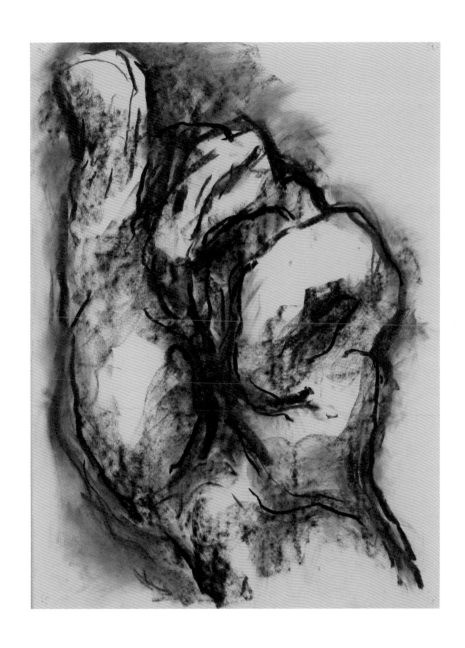

(ABOVE)
Vermont C
2004, Charcoal
on Paper
76 x 56 cm

(RIGHT)
Study for 'Gift'
2004, Bronze
Edition of 6
15.2 cm high

Set of Four Hands
2009, Bronze
Edition of 10
5-7cm high

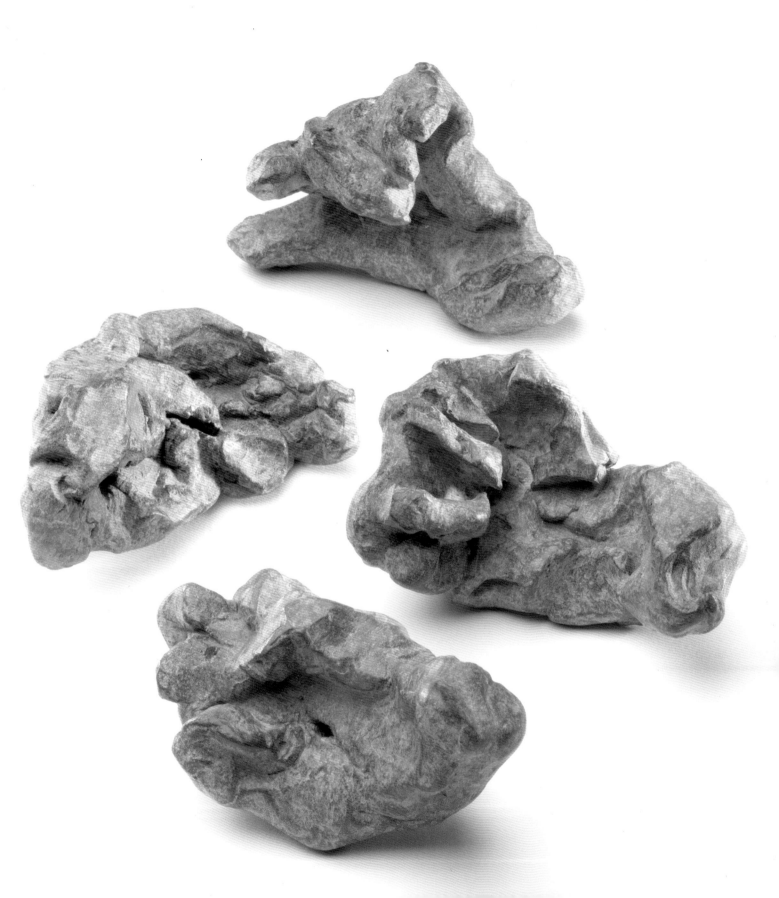

Study for 'The Void'
2004, Bronze
Edition of 6
11 cm high

Study for 'The Secret'
2004, Bronze
Edition of 6
11 cm high

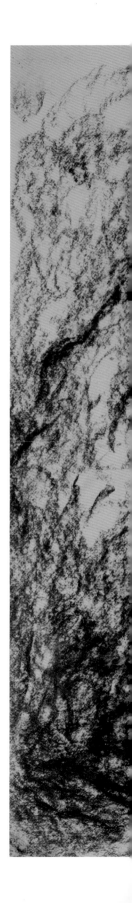

Study for 'Tauromachy'
2007, Charcoal
on Paper
81 x 101.5 cm

Study for 'Dreamer'
1991, Bronze
Edition of 6
13.3 cm high

(ABOVE)
Greek Horse
2003, Bronze
Edition of 4
142.2 cm high

(RIGHT)
Horse Drawing I
2003, Charcoal
on paper
90 x 76 cm

(ABOVE)
Messenger
2001, Bronze
Edition of 3
320 cm high

(RIGHT)
Study for 'Messenger'
2000, Charcoal
on paper
76 x 57 cm

Study for 'Dancer'
2002 Bronze
Edition of 6
17 cm high

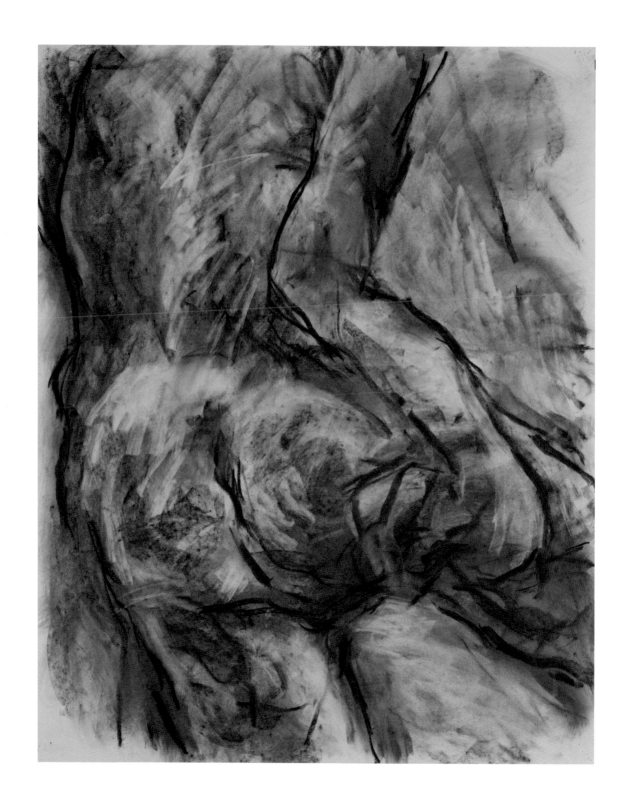

(LEFT)
Study for 'Dancer' I
2003, Charcoal
on paper
101.5 x 81.5 cm

(ABOVE)
Dancer After Degas
2002, Sterling Silver
Edition of 10
13.5 cm high

Study for 'Dancer' II
2003, Charcoal
on paper
101.5 x 81 cm

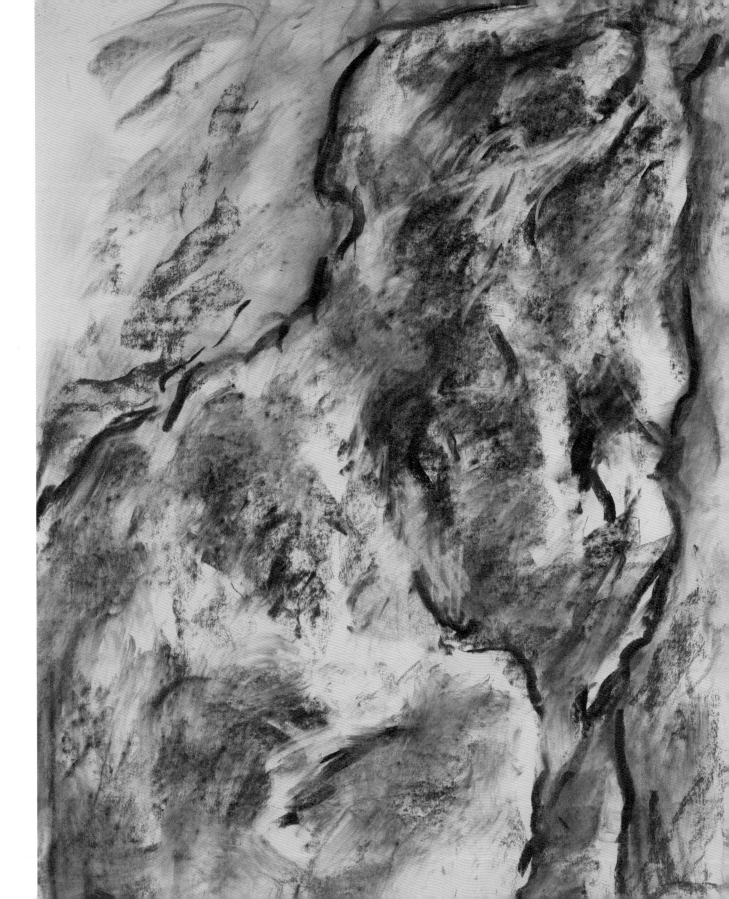

(RIGHT)
Monoprint I
1987
Monoprint
75 × 57 cm

(CLOCKWISE FROM
TOP LEFT)
Monoprint XVIII
Monoprint XIX
Monoprint VII
Monoprint XX
1987
Monoprint
75 × 57 cm

Study for 'Pomona'
1999, Bronze
Edition of 6
15.2 cm high

Siren
1994, Bronze
Edition of 4
94 cm high

WILLIAM TUCKER

BIOGRAPHY

1935	Born, Cairo, Egypt (to English parents)
1937	Family returns to England
1955-58	Studies at Oxford University
1959-60	Studies at Central School of Art and Design and St. Martin's School of Art, London
1962-66	Teaches at Goldsmith's College, London
1963-74	Teaches at St. Martin's School of Art, London
1968-70	Receives Gregory Fellowship in Sculpture, Leeds University
1976	Teaches at University of West Ontario, Canada
1977	Teaches at Nova Scotia College of Art and Design, Halifax, Canada
1978-92	Teaches at New York Studio School of Painting and Sculpture, New York
1978-82	Teaches at Columbia University, New York
1980-81	Receives Guggenheim Fellowship
1986	Becomes American Citizen
	Receives National Endowment for the Arts Fellowship
1991	Receives International Sculpture Center Award for Distinction in Sculpture
1993	Appointed Co-Chairman of the Art Department of Bard College
1995	Receives Rodin-Moore Memorial Prize, Second Fujisankei Biennale Hakone Open-Air Museum, Japan
1996	Receives commission for large-scale sculpture for Bilbao, Spain
1999	Receives award from New York Studio School, New York
2010	Receives Lifetime Achievement Award from the International Sculpture Center

SELECTED SOLO EXHIBITIONS

2008	*Affinities*, McKee Gallery, New York, NY
2006-7	*William Tucker: Horses*, DeCordova Museum and Sculpture Park, Lincoln, MA
2004	*William Tucker, Sculpture & Drawings*, Gallery Paule Anglim, San Francisco, CA
	William Tucker: Recent Sculpture, McKee Gallery, New York
2003	*Drawings by William Tucker, Arts on the Point*, Healey Library Gallery, University of Massachusetts, Boston
2002	*William Tucker: New Sculpture*, McKee Gallery, New York
2001	*William Tucker*, Tate Gallery, Liverpool
	William Tucker, Yorkshire Sculpture Park, Wakefield, UK
1999	*William Tucker: Drawings and Sculpture*, Davidson College, Davidson, North Carolina

1999	Gallery Paule Anglim, San Francisco
	McKee Gallery, New York
1996	McKee Gallery, New York
1994	McKee Gallery, New York
1993	*The Philosophers, Sculpture and Drawings 1989-1992* , Maak Gallery, London
1992	*New Drawings,* McKee Gallery, New York
1991	David McKee Gallery, New York
1989	*William Tucker,* The Art Museum, Florida International University, Miami, FL
	Gallery Paule Anglim, San Francisco
1987	*Gods: Five Recent Sculptures,* Tate Gallery, London
1985	Neuberger Museum, SUNY, Purchase, NY
	Pamela Auchincloss Gallery, Santa Barbara
	David McKee Gallery, New York
1984	David McKee Gallery, New York
	L'Isola Gallery, Rome, Italy
1980	David Reids Gallery, Sydney, Australia
	Robert Elkon Gallery, New York

SELECTED GROUP EXHIBITIONS

2007	*British Visions: Modern and Contemporary Sculpture and Words on Paper,* Davidson College, Davidson, North Carolina
	Small Bodies, McKee Gallery, New York, NY
2006	*Against the Grain: Contemporary Art from the Edward R. Broida Collection,* The Museum of Modern Art, New York, NY
2004	*The 179th Annual: An Invitational Exhibition of Contemporary American Art,* National Academy Museum, New York, NY
2002	*Sculpture,* Robert Steele Gallery, New York, NY
	Tra-la-la: British Sculpture in the Sixties, Duveen Galleries, Tate Britain, London
2000-01	*Bronze: Contemporary British Sculpture,* Holland Park, London and Sculpture at Goodwood, West Sussex
	The Concealed Space, British Sculpture, Associazione Piemontese Arte, Turin
	NEW works, McKee Gallery, New York
2001	*Kinds of Drawing,* Herter Art Gallery, University of Massachusetts, Amherst, MA
2000	*American Academy Invitational Exhibition of Painting & Sculpture,* The American Academy of Arts and Letters, New York
1999	*House of Sculpture,* Modern Art Museum of Fort Worth, Texas: travelled to Museo de Arte Contemporaneo, Monterrey, Mexico
	New Sculpture, McKee Gallery, New York, NY
1998	*The Edward R. Broida Collection,* Orlando Museum of Art, Orlando, FL
1997	*Sculptors' Drawings,* The Visual Arts Museum, The School of Visual Arts, New York, NY

1997	*Currents of Modern Sculpture,* Two Sculptors, Inc., New York, NY
	Reconfigurations, Pamela Auchincloss, New York, NY
1996	*From Figure to Object: A Century of Sculptors' Drawings,* Frith Street Gallery and Karsten Schubert, London
1995	*Twentieth Century American Sculpture at The White House,* First Ladies' Garden, The White House, Washington, D.C.
	Critical Mass, Yale University School of Art, New Haven, CT & The MAC, Dallas, TX
	Contemporary British Sculpture: From Henry Moore to the 90's, Auditoria de Galicia, Santiago, Chile
1994	*American Academy Invitational Exhibition of Painting & Sculpture,* The American Academy of Arts and Letters, NY
	Art Partners, Gallery at Park West, Kingston, NY
1993	*Hyper Cathexis: Layers of Experience,* Stux Gallery, New York
	Small Works Sculpture Show, Robert Morrison Gallery, New York
1992	Panicali Fine Art, New York
1991	*Steel and Wood ,* Philippe Staib Gallery, New York
	ArtPark, The Art Museum, Florida International University, Miami, FL
1990	*The Art of Drawing,* Lehman College Art Gallery, Bronx, NY
1988	*From the Southern Cross: A View of World Art c. 1940-1988,* Australian Biennale, Art Gallery of New South Wales
1987	*New York Beijing: 22 American Artists / Works on Paper,* Beijing Art Institute, China
1986	*Recent Acquisitions,* Museum of Modern Art, New York, NY
	Opening Exhibition, Socrates Sculpture Park, Long Island City, New York, NY

SELECTED COLLECTIONS

Aberdeen Art Gallery, Scotland
Art Gallery of New South Wales, Sydney, Australia
Arts Council of Great Britain, London
British Council, London
British Museum, London
City of Bilbao, Spain
Contemporary Art Society, London
Florida International University, Miami, FL
Solomon R. Guggenheim Museum, New York
Hakone - Open Air Museum, Tokyo, Japan
Hirshhorn Museum and Sculpture Garden, Washington, D.C.
Louisiana Museum of Modern Art, Humlebaek, Denmark
Martin Z. Margulies Sculpture Park, Florida International University, Miami, FL
Metropolitan Museum of Art, New York
The Museum of Modern Art, New York

National Gallery of Victoria, Melbourne, Australia
Rijksmuseum Kroller-Muller, Otterlo, Holland
Rose Art Museum, Brandeis University, Waltham, MA
Storm King Art Center, Mountainville, NY
Peter Stuyvesant Foundation, Newcastle-upon-Tyne, England
Tate Gallery, London
University of California at Los Angeles
Victoria and Albert Museum, London
Walker Art Center, Minneapolis

INSTALLATIONS

2006	*Six Bronzes*: Ward Pound Ridge Reservation, Cross River, NY
2001	*Victory 1981*: Parque de la Memoria, Buenos Aires, Argentina (permanent)
2000	*Rites of Spring 2000*: Long House Reserve, East Hampton, NY
1999	*Important Sculptors of the Late Twentieth Century,* Stamford Sculpture Walk, Stamford, CT
1998	*Frenhofer*: Goodwood Sculpture Park, England
	Maia, Riverside Sculpture Park, Abandoibarra, Bilbao, Spain (permanent)
1997	*Vishnu*: Neuberger Museum of Art Biennial Exhibition for Public Art , Neuberger Museum, SUNY Purchase, New York
1991	*Prometheus*: M. H. de Young Memorial Museum and California Palace of the Legion of *Honor*: Lincoln Park, (Permanently installed at Runnymede Sculpture Park, Menlo, CA)
1989	*Okeanos*: Scripps Clinic and Research Foundation, LaJolla (permanent)
1988-91	*The Rim*: The Art Museum, Florida International University, Miami, FL
1987	*The Rim*: Laumeier Sculpture Park, St. Louis, MO
1986	*Rhea*: Greenwich Plaza, Greenwich, CT (permanent)
	Gymnast II: The Museum of Modern Art, New York
1984	*Arc and Fear*: Springs Mills Building at Citicorp Center, New York
	Guardian I: Saint Peter's Church at Citicorp Center, New York
1983	*Victory*: Doris C. Freedman Plaza, Fifth Avenue at 6oth Street, New York
1982-83	*Journey:* Dag Hammarskjold Plaza, New York
1982	*The Promise*: Grove Isle Sculpture Garden, Miami, FL (permanent)
1980	*The Rim*: The Mall, Washington, D.C.
1976	*Angel:* Livingston Development Corporation, Lanark, Scotland (permanent)
1972	Peter Stuyvesant Sculpture Project, Newcastle-upon-Tyne, England

SELECTED PUBLICATIONS

The Language of Sculpture by William Tucker, Thames & Hudson, London, 1974
The Sculpture of William Tucker by Joy Sleeman, The Henry Moore Foundation, Lund Humphries, 2007

ACKNOWLEDGEMENTS

This exhibition is the culmination of almost two years work to bring about the creation of a number of William Tucker's sculptures in their intended medium of cast bronze.

During this time a number of people have worked extremely hard to make the exhibition come to fruition and we would like to take this opportunity to thank William Tucker and his family, Steve Maule and his highly skilled team at Pangolin Editions, Keith Patrick for his insightful and erudite essay and Steve Russell for his excellent photography.

PHOTO CREDITS

Pangolin London would like to thank the following for kindly allowing us to reproduce a number of images:
Beulah I, p.5, Courtesy of the Artist/Tate Collection
Tunnel, p. 6, Courtesy of the Artist/Tate Collection
Carytid, p. 9, Courtesy of the Artist/McKee Gallery

Printed to coincide with the exhibition:
William Tucker: Sculpture & Drawing
10th March - 24th April 2010
Pangolin London
Kings Place, 90 York Way, London, N1 9AG
T: 020 7520 1480
E: gallery@pangolinlondon.com

Printed in Century Gothic & Corbel
Designed by Pangolin London
Photography by Steve Russell
Printed by Healeys Printers

Mixed Sources
Product group from well-managed forests and other controlled sources
www.fsc.org Cert no. SGS-COC-004497
© 1996 Forest Stewardship Council
FSC